ADVENT

A Journey Of Waiting, Watching And Preparing For The Light

Erik E. Willits

ADVENT: A Journey Of Waiting,
Watching And Preparing For The Light

Copyright © 2013 by Erik E. Willits

Publisher: Mark Oestreicher
Managing Editor: Anne Marie Miller
Cover Design: Adam McLane
Layout: Marilee R. Pankratz
Creative Director: Buddy the Elf

ISBN-13: 9780988741393
ISBN-10: 0988741393

The Youth Cartel, LLC
www.theyouthcartel.com
Email: info@theyouthcartel.com
Born in San Diego
Printed in the U.S.A.

To my pastor, John Hollis, who retired in 2013 after 37 years of ministry at my home church, Freeport Church of the Nazarene in Freeport, Illinois. You and your family have taught me to prepare and participate in the Kingdom of heaven, and I am eternally grateful.

And to Andrea, I couldn't do it without you.

Table of Contents

Welcome to a Journey of Discovery – page 2

How to Use This Book – page 5

WAIT – page 8

PREPARE – page 17

HOPE – page 28

AWAKE – page 36

CHRISTMASTIDE – page 46

EPIPHANY – page 62

Notes – page 65

Welcome to a Journey of Discovery

Advent is the time of year that prepares us for Christmas, the birth of our savior Jesus Christ. It's a period when we learn to wait, watch, hope and prepare for His coming. In fact, Advent is the first date on the church calendar, beginning the year for Christ followers. I haven't always worshiped in a tradition that embraced the church calendar, but recently I learned to embrace this method of keeping time.

In the same way our culture uses a calendar to track important dates — celebrating and remembering things that have happened in the past — the church calendar moves us through the year and encourages us to focus on important moments, dates and seasons in the life of God's people.

Both calendars share events like Christmas and Easter to an extent, but the church is called to embrace these events and holidays differently than we celebrate them in the culture at large. One of the biggest differences is where we begin. Our culture starts the year off on January 1, but Christians take a different route. Christmas, the birth of Christ, the incarnation of God—which is the story of God taking on skin and moving into our neighborhood—is the central idea for Christians. We could just kick off our calendar year here with a big Christmas party but because we are more concerned with spiritual formation than convenience (or even common sense), we need to be ready for this party so we start our year with the first Sunday of Advent.

With that said, let me be the first to wish you a "Happy New Year!"

I also want to welcome you to a counter-cultural way of celebrating Christ's birth, a way of subversion (or overthrowing the norm by living a new version of the story) and insurrection (or rebellion from the inside out). After all, Jesus' means of changing the world is to place himself on the inside and work out his plan from there. This is what Advent and Christmastide are all about.

The way we'll learn to celebrate these stories might be different from how you've done it in the past. That's because our culture does celebrate a variation of Advent and almost everyone celebrates Christmas. The celebrations we are familiar with centers mainly around purchasing and consuming. Gift giving and card writing are the significance of the season. It's such a stressful and debt-ridden time of year that people wind up depressed and stressed to the max.

Christians do things a bit differently. We don't encourage you to be counter-cultural or subversive on your own. This is not a trendy fad with a T-shirt and clever slogan. It's the opposite, actually. This journey might seclude you a bit. It might wind up making you look like a wanderer in a foreign land. Advent literally means, "coming," so Christians spend a few weeks waiting and preparing for that which comes, namely God Himself. Joan Chittister in her book *The Liturgical Year*, tells us "Advent is about learning to wait." That's because waiting is a key part of our spiritual formation. She says, "It is waiting that attunes us to the invisible in a highly material world."

Our church calendar and Christ both invite us to this different way of living, to a different way of celebrating and ultimately to a different way of keeping time.

For us, patience and prayer mark Advent. Waiting is the hallmark of our Advent season. We learn to be people who wait for what we know God will do. But hasn't Jesus already arrived? Why do we wait and prepare for him again? Think of it like flashbacks in a movie. They pull you into a part of the story that you already know the ending to, but you wind up so engrossed in the narrative that you relive the moments as if the end hasn't even happened. We get so caught up in retelling and reliving the story of God's people through characters like Mary and Joseph, Elizabeth, John, the wise men, the shepherds and other people that we almost forget that Christ has already been born.

Advent also encourages us to be formed by the ideas of waiting, preparing and hoping as the characters in our Advent story teach us what it looks like to live these things as we wait for Christ's second coming. With this in mind, we realize that all of life is an Advent. We are always waiting. That's why this time of year is so very important and formative. Most of us aren't very good at waiting. Advent gives us practice and, with the help of the Holy Spirit, teaches us to wait upon the Lord in all the moments of our lives.

That brings us to Christmastide. This is a fancy way to talk about not only Christmas Day and the culmination of our waiting and preparing, but also the twelve days when we celebrate Christ's birth and incarnation. That's right, we get twelve days of Christmas — not just one! As we get into the Christmastide devotions, you will hopefully begin to realize the depth and texture, the beauty that these twelve days lead us through.

The idea for this guide to Advent and Christmastide is that you will enter into this journey with your church, youth group, small group or family. The journey of learning to wait, prepare and hope shouldn't be done alone. Ultimately, it should stir in you the desire to help the poor and give to those in need. It should encourage you to walk and not run and pray instead of purchase. Having people with you on the journey will help you to do all these things well.

I hope this book you hold in your hands helps you and your community along the way as you wait patiently on the Lord this Advent season.

How to Use This Book...

With Advent and Christmastide together, we are embarking on a journey that will last about 40 days. Here's how it works.

This book is comprised of scripture readings, reflections and questions for every day of the journey. Each day, you'll engage the different readings whether you're participating with your family, in a group or if you prefer reading them in your own time. Our journey will begin on the fourth Sunday before Christmas Day, which is always the first Sunday of Advent. It will end twelve days after Christmas as we are launched into the season of Epiphany.

Each week is grouped into Advent and Christmastide themes like *Wait, Prepare, Hope* and *Awake*. Each week will give you biblical characters and stories to frame your week and set an example for you to study and explore the given theme, drawing you deeper into the journey.

Christmastide gets a bit tricky. You have to stay awake for its arrival. Every year Christmas comes on a different day of the week. As you are reading through Week Four of this book, Christmas Day happens. When it does, skip a few pages and turn to the Christmastide section of the book. If there are extra days you didn't read, make note and come back to them on days when you need a little extra encouragement, or a reminder that God is always on His way.

Every day of the week will start off with a Bible reading. This scripture has been intentionally left out of this book so that you can engage with the passage in your own Bible. Highlight the passage, take notes, doodle...use the physical pages in your Bible as part of the journey. It may be easy to skip over this part and head straight into the devotion. I encourage you to take the extra minute or two, sit down with your Bible and read the Scripture for the day. If you only do one thing, do this.

After the Scripture, you'll find a brief devotional thought and also a meditation from a writer, scholar, thinker or interesting person. All of these things will help you think more deeply about that week's theme. They can be challenging—including some big theological words and maybe ideas you haven't thought about before— but don't be discouraged. If you don't understand something, ask someone in your community or a parent, and you can even email me (my information is included in the back of the book). I would love to listen to your questions and help you find answers.

On Sundays, you will find four Scripture readings from the Lectionary, a list of scripture readings churches all over the world use for their worship services. Reading the same Scriptures as thousands of other Christians around the world helps us remember that we are a part of something amazing and big. We are not alone on this journey.

There are also a few traditional practices I would encourage you to participate in with your community and your family during Advent.

The Advent Calendar

Often Advent calendars are full of little chocolate gifts that count down to the big gifts we will receive on Christmas Day. Many of them start on December 1, but we will start our calendar whenever the first Sunday of Advent falls. You may want to make your own calendar that will produce anticipation and expectation in your life and help you and your family and community engage in this period of waiting and preparing. Check out the Advent Web Guide for some inspiration, or head over to Pinterest for countless Advent calendar ideas.

Keep in mind that we want to find creative ways to flip the script on the Advent calendar idea, making it about something more than getting chocolate gifts before one big gift on Christmas. We want to make our daily advent challenges about giving a note to a friend, a donation to a non-profit, or a small anonymous gift or encouragement. If you're extra motivated, make one of these challenges for every day in advance. We'll also have some creative challenges and ideas posted for you on the Web Guide. Stay tuned, and stay connected.

The Advent Wreath

A predominant image for Advent and Christmastide is that of light—a great light coming into the world. One way that Christian communities embrace this imagery is to make traditional Advent wreaths.

Advent wreaths consist of five candles in a green wreath. Some people choose four red candles and one white candle, traditional Christmas colors, but a lot of Christian traditions use three purple candles, one rose-colored candle and one white candle. After constructing their wreath, families and communities gather around it to light one candle each week of the Advent journey, with the final white candle being lit on Christmas morning.

Visit the Advent Web Guide for more details on the Advent wreath tradition including what the significance of the colors is.

The Advent Web Guide is a supplement to this book. There, you will find images and icons, videos, more great meditative quotes and Bible reading, as well as an opportunity to leave comments, ask questions and share a bit of your journey through this time of Advent.

www.AdventWebGuide.com

As you're reading, look for these icons.

SNAP!
There's a picture, image or Christian icon
for you to check out!

You're only a click away.
We've posted a link to a website, blog or
something cool for you to look at!

We've got a great video, YouTube,
Vimeo or other goodie for you to watch.

Listen up!
We've posted an audio clip, sermon
or message for you to listen to!

We like the Bible around here!
When you see this, we've got more
Scripture for you!

Get ready to be inspired!
We've posted a quote or meditation
that you won't want to miss.

There's an app for that.
We've provided a link to an app for your smart
phone that might help you on this journey.

It's time to experiment!
Get ready to experiment with living
out what you're learning!

WAIT

ADVENT SUNDAY #1
WAIT — DAY 1

| Isaiah 64:1-9 | 1 Corinthians 1:3-9 |
| Psalm 80:1-7, 16-18 | Mark 13:24-37 |

Our Sunday readings are from the Revised Common Lectionary, year B. If your community follows the lectionary, make sure you check which lectionary year is being followed. The resource on the Advent Web Guide can help you with this. My hope is that you read these verses, meditate on them and engage them on Sunday morning with your church community. If your church doesn't follow the Lectionary, it's still powerful to know that thousands of Christians around the world are reading and thinking about these same verses. You're a part of something big: You're not on this journey alone!

I use a few key resources to help me connect to the Lectionary, Bible reading and the church calendar during this season. Check out the Lent Web Guide to get your hands on these resources.

WAIT // DAY 2
READING :: Luke 1:5-25

The story that frames our first week of Advent reflects many of the stories we find in the scriptures—a godly couple waiting, longing, and pleading for a child. The wife is barren, the husband is old, and waiting has turned into doubt, despair and disgrace.

Why are these stories so prevalent in the scriptures? Why does the theme of a holy longing and a perpetual waiting occur so frequently? It's human nature. We all want it—whatever "it" happens to be—*now*. Nobody wants to wait. If the Bible does anything, it tells a real story of a real people. And if you've ever deeply engaged the scriptures, you quickly realized that their story is our story. We have all found ourselves waiting. You can probably remember a time in the last week when you were in a waiting room or waiting in line. Waiting is a part of life and we do it a lot.

I wonder how many of us wait like Sarah and Zechariah in today's reading. Over the years, Zechariah fell in such despair and doubt because of the wait that God gave him that he questioned the angel that appeared to him. Let me repeat that: The *angel* that *appeared* to him.

We all have given up hope on some level, haven't we? We've moved on and written off God's promise. Even Elizabeth says in Luke 1:25 that she had translated her wait into disgrace instead of grace. When God finally answered her prayers for a child, she realized her status as favored in His sight. It's not that she wasn't favored when she was waiting; she was always favored but let doubt destroy her confidence.

Like Zechariah and Elizabeth, we often let waiting produce doubt when God intends for waiting to produce faith, hope and love.

Our challenge in Advent is to embrace the wait as a gift and not as a curse, to see in all our moments of waiting that God is preparing us for the good He has in store. Our wait is a grace, not a disgrace—if we have eyes to see all God wants to do in and through our time of waiting.

Can you think of a time when you let your waiting become doubt or disgrace?

Meditation ::.

"Personal prayer is the meeting place between the Eternal One and me; the Blessed Sacrament is the visible sign of my covenant with him.

That is why I believe in personal prayer, and why every day I wait to meet him in the Eucharist. To pray means to wait for the God who comes.

Every prayer-filled day sees a meeting with the God who comes; every night that we faithfully put at his disposal is full of his presence.

And his coming and his presence are not only the result of our waiting or a prize for our efforts: they are his decision, based on his love freely poured out.

His coming is bound to his promise, not to our works or virtue. We have not earned the meeting with God because we have served him faithfully in our brethren, or because we have heaped up such a pile of virtue as to shine before Heaven.

God is thrust onward by his love, not attracted by our beauty. He comes even in moments when we have done everything wrong, when we have done nothing... when we have sinned."

The God Who Comes, Carlo Carretto

In college, I had a theology professor who was famous for his prayers. Before I ever attended his class, I heard lore of his one- or two-line prayers that went something like this: "Crucify us. In the name of the Father, Son and Holy Spirit. Amen." When I finally sat in his classroom and had the opportunity to pray with him, all the rumors were true, but the thing that struck me most about his unsettling prayers was the space he left after "Let us pray" and before the first words of the prayer. In reality, it was only 30 seconds or maybe a minute. But those 30 seconds of silent waiting felt so long and awkward that I wanted to open my eyes and see if something was wrong. My ears naturally tuned in to the sounds and the breathing around me and strained to hear if anything was happening. I thought I was waiting to hear a prayer—waiting to pray.

In reality, the space my professor was creating with this silence and waiting was itself prayer. And my natural response to tune into the silence and listen for all that was happening is exactly what Advent is all about.

Have you ever thought about waiting and silence as prayer?

Meditation ::.

"Biblically, waiting is not just something we have to do until we get what we want. Waiting is part of the process of becoming what God wants us to be."

The Life You Always Wanted: Spiritual Disciplines for Ordinary People, John Ortberg

The minute you pick up an Advent resource like this one, you probably expect to hear a list of creative ways you can get ready for Christmas. Or how you can have the right biblical perspective on the days leading up to the birth of Christ, preparing yourself not for presents but for "presence," for Jesus. That's surely a large part of Advent, and we'll get there in time, but for now, I want us to deepen our perspective on waiting, which is at the heart of our Advent journey.

Like I did in my college professor's class, we often forget to embrace the space God has given us to wait. We think of waiting as something to get through. But I'd like to suggest that waiting isn't done because something is wrong or because the action isn't happening yet. Waiting is the gift God gives us so our senses and spirits can be tuned in to all that He is doing and going to do. This is the space created when we meditate or practice the discipline of silence. As we talked about yesterday, the space of waiting is the prayer as much as the words we use in prayer. The waiting of Advent, the begging and pleading we do with the mantra, "Come, Lord Jesus, come," is maybe as important to our souls as the days of fulfillment and thanksgiving we will experience during Christmastide.

Embrace your wait. Let your ears and hearts open to the breath of God and His whispers of love as you wait for the presence of God in the Christ Child. Be fully present in the waiting instead of only looking forward to the fulfillment.

How can you create space in your own life
to wait on the Lord this Advent?

I once heard a story of a remote village in Africa that was over an hour away from the nearest water source. The women and families of the village would spend hours each day trekking back and forth to provide water for their families to live.

In our culture of instant gratification, where water is never more than a minute away, our response to this is: "THEY NEED A WELL!" If these people just had a water source in their community, it would fix all their problems.

An organization came in and dug a well in this remote village, and the people loved it! Water was immediately accessible. No more waiting, no more traveling and so much more time for other things. The organization left, feeling satisfied that they had helped to provide clean and sustainable water for the village, meeting a need and living out their mission.

A year later, the organization returned to check on the village. The first thing the villagers asked was if the organization could take away the well because they no longer wanted it. Shocked, the organization couldn't understand why they would ever want to get rid of this instant source of water that took away the waiting and the work. But as the organization probed deeper into this peculiar response, they begin to realize the value of instant water had removed other values the community had long embraced: waiting, working, walking together and the like. The villagers had realized that much of their life, learning and loving of one another happened as they waited, worked and walked together down the road to water. That was lost with their new well.

This Advent, what do we lose because we have largely removed waiting from our lives? When is the last time you went on a long walk by yourself or with a friend? When is the last time you took the back, country roads instead of the interstate? What would happen if you waited to answer your email in the morning and instead, sat on your back patio and listened to the wind, waves and the whisper of God all around you?

What do we lose in our pursuit to remove waiting from our lives?

Meditation ::.

"The one who loves, who abides, continually emancipates himself from the past. He knows no past; he is only waiting for the future.

Does the dance end because one of the dancers has gone away? In a certain sense. But if the other remains standing in the position that expresses bowing toward the one who is not seen, and if you know nothing about the past, you will say, "the dance will surely begin just as soon as the other one, who is awaited, comes."

Get rid of the past, drown it in the oblivion of eternity by abiding in love— then the end is the beginning, and there is no break!"

Works of Love, Soren Kierkegaard

Kierkegaard here encourages us on our Advent journey to wait in a very particular way. We are to wait like the dancer, confident in her partner's return. We are to wait in a way that does not despair in the past but waits with a posture of readiness as if there is no waiting at all.

A huge part of our Advent journey is the remembering of how we wait for the Christ child but just as important is that we wait for his return. We wait like the dancer, ready to pick up as if there was no wait at all. It's simply one long dance.

Are you waiting in such a way that it looks like you're ready
at any moment to dance?

Just to be sure we understand Advent waiting I want to clarify something: The kind of waiting we do during Advent isn't passive; it's not a couch potato kind of waiting. Instead, it's the waiting of the backup quarterback who practices, prepares and lives in such a way that you would think he is the starter. Or it's the mother who eagerly waits for her child to be born. While she's waiting, she's taking birthing classes, getting the nursery ready and scouring every corner of the house. The way both the backup quarterback and the pregnant woman wait is by taking action.

Our Advent waiting is an active waiting, not a passive waiting.

There is a tension here, however. We can easily live as if we aren't waiting for anything at all, but we can also drift into a laziness that might look like waiting…but it's actually resignation, a giving up on what you thought was coming. Filling your moments of waiting with too much work or with excessive sloth are not the rhythms of a healthy Advent.

As we wait for the coming Christ, his birth and his return, we wait in a way that is active but also engaged in silence and stillness that we find in our days. We wait in a way that makes room in our lives for our participation with Christ. We don't wait on the couch; we wait on our knees, and we wait with our service to the poor and struggling. We realize the Christ who is coming hopes for a space to be cleared for his arrival in our hearts, our homes and our neighborhoods.

Check out the Advent Web Guide, and you'll find a video where Rowan Williams says, "Waiting seems negative, passive, unexciting, the boring bit before we get to the exciting bit." Let that not be true of us. This Advent, let's wait in silence and prayer, with action and stillness. In all of this we wait all the same on our coming light, Jesus Christ.

How do you wait?
What are practices of healthy Advent waiting?

PREPARE

ADVENT :: SUNDAY 2

Isaiah 40:1-11	2 Peter 3:8-15a
Psalm 85:1-2, 8-13	Mark 1:1-8

John the Baptist is our Advent portrait of preparation! He's our icon, if you will—the image that points us to the greater reality God is leading us into.

In Matthew's account, John is painted as a peculiar prophet, wearing a camel hair coat with a sweet leather belt to complete his outfit. He dines on bugs and wild honey—exotic, right? Now, don't worry, the takeaway from the life of John the Baptist isn't to eat exotic bugs and wear fur coats and leather belts (unless you want to). What we learn from John the Baptist is that living a life prepared for the Messiah means looking a little peculiar to the culture around you.

Do we as Christians look any different in the way we participate in Advent and prepare for the birth of Christ than the rest of our culture? In my observation, many times those who believe in Jesus and those who don't participate in Advent in a similar way—by hanging lots of lights and buying lots of gifts. In fact, the majority of Christians I know prepare for Christmas, which means participating in Advent, by preparing to give and receive presents and have Christmas parties. Don't get me wrong, I love a good Christmas party as much as the next guy, but I don't want that to be primary marker of my Advent experience.

This is why the way of John the Baptist and the Advent he lives is so radical and counter-cultural. As we authentically engage the Advent portrayed by John the Baptist, our response should be the same as those who listened to him in Luke 3: "What should we do?" And John tells us. "If you have two coats, give one away and do the same with your food." He then talks to different people with different influences and abilities and helps each of them with a practical way to prepare for the coming of the Christ and His Kingdom.

Why not take a moment and evaluate your gifts, abilities, possessions and circles of influence? Bring a friend, parent or pastor into the conversation and come up with a "John the Baptist" approach. Meaning, if John were to look at your life, what kind of practical challenge would he give you this Advent, as you prepare for the coming of Jesus in His birth, His return and in the coming of His Kingdom on earth?

How would John the Baptist challenge you
to prepare for Jesus this Advent?

Meditation ::.

"Centuries of church history... have taught us to misunderstand radically what John the Baptist and Jesus meant when they began preaching, "Repent! For the kingdom is at hand!" Under "repentance" we think of remorse, regret, sorrow for sin. But what they were calling for was a transformation of understanding (metanoia), a redirected will ready to live in a new kind of world."

The Original Revolution, John Howard Yoder

Reflecting on what we learned yesterday, Advent preparedness is a call to justice, a call to bring heaven to earth, to participate in the coming of the Kingdom on earth as it is in heaven. In order to accomplish this, John the Baptist centers his Advent life on the idea of repentance. Repentance is essentially a turning, specifically a turning or changing of our minds about how we live life.

John the Baptist and Jesus were both calling people to change their minds about how they were living and preparing for the Kingdom of God. We all know how difficult it can be to change our minds once they're made up. We hold our beliefs close to our hearts, especially religious traditions and values. When those are threatened, we often refuse to consider other options.

At the heart of John the Baptist's preparedness, however, was a thinking that is transformational for our culture of consumption, greed and gift exchange. He urged conformity to a Kingdom of generosity and justice in preparing for Christ's coming. He advocated for feeding the poor and clothing the naked, loving the broken and calling out the self-righteous. All was in an attempt to make straight a path for the Lord.

John was preparing the way for the Lord Jesus to return, quite literally. He probably didn't know when or how exactly, but he knew it was happening. If there needed to be some refining fires (see Matthew 3:10-11, Malachi 3:3) on Jesus' arrival, there would be, but John hoped to live in a way that prepared him and others for the great event.

The way we participate in Advent is usually very different from John the Baptist's way. But he is calling us to repent—to rethink the way we do it.

How can you prepare with generosity and justice
rather than greed and gifts?

Meditation ::.

"We are still waiting to see what might happen if Jesus is allowed into our lives that bit more fully, that bit more radically. So again for Christians Advent is a time when they do a bit of self-examination; have I allowed Jesus in yet, has the good news really made the full impact it might make or is my life still locked into old patterns, into darkness, in slavery, into being not at home with myself or God or with other people? It's a time of self-examination, repentance indeed, facing myself honestly and saying sorry for the things that don't easily face the light."
Rowan Williams[1]

During Advent, we wait and prepare for the light of Christ to come into the world. And when it does, we know that everything will be exposed. All that we are called to be will be, and everything we've every done will be put on display. This is what God does with the birth of his son Jesus, and what he will do again when he comes to judge the living and the dead. During Advent, we wait and prepare, watch and get ready for this great light to enter our great darkness.

Rowan Williams helps us understand that Advent is a season when we are supposed to confront the darkness around us and inside us—the darkness of tempting despair, the darkness of hopelessness about a world where there is so much cruelty and so much meaninglessness. But that also means getting in touch with something else inside us, the longing and desire, the urge for something better, fuller, more joyful.

As believers, we do not hide from the light, uncomfortable as it may be. We believe the light comes to reveal truth and heal us. So we pray, "Come, Lord Jesus, come," and we wait, watch and prepare for the light to come.

If I shone a spotlight on your life, what would be exposed?
How might you prepare your heart
for the light to expose all the corners of your life?

Does our Christmas preparation reflect our preparation for Christ's return? We prepare for Christmas with lights and lots of action. We purchase heaps of stuff, expecting we will get heaps of stuff in return. In America, we prepare for Christmas by giving and receiving gifts, which are often connected to the giving and receiving of love. The more you give, the more you love, or so society thinks.

Confession: I was—not just once, but on a regular basis—upset because I didn't receive the gift I wanted. I've measured people's care for me by the gifts they gave me. I've been guilty of having conversations like, "How much are you going to spend on me? I want to make sure I spend as much on you." Many of us use this time of year as a gauge for love and try to prove our love for others with the gifts we give.

Is this how you are preparing for Christ's return?

Do you gauge Christ's love for you by what He has given you, or what you feel He has withheld from you? Do you try to prove your love for Him by how much you put in an offering plate or how many church services you attend? Do you try to exchange your service for God's gifts and even His love? Perhaps you are ultimately trying to earn or at least prove yourself worthy of your spot in His kingdom when He returns.

John the Baptist calls us to repent, and I would suggest this is the very thinking we must repent from.

Maybe this Advent, we need to cut the strings attached to our gifts, give without agenda and receive with pure gratitude. Maybe this Advent, we need to prepare by giving more, getting rid of excess and finding ways to love without expectation. We can prepare by participating now in the kingdom that is coming. We can prepare by praying "Thy kingdom come; Thy will be done on earth as it is in heaven." Then, by the grace of God, we can work alongside Him to answer our prayers in part until they're fully answered with His second coming.

This Advent, let's place our expectation in the coming Christ, the ultimate gift and sign of unconditional love.

How might you cut the strings of conditional love
and gift-giving this Advent?

Have you ever heard the phrase, "What you win them with, you win them to"? Folks usually use it to talk about ministry programs and church services. Basically, if you use games and lots of fun as your means to attract friends and somebody passing by to your youth group or church, and then preach a 10-minute message at the end telling them about Jesus, you are really winning them with games and fun. If you ever try to change that formula, it will be difficult, because what you win them with (games, emotional worship, relationships, great sermons, etc.), you win them to. This isn't meant to be a negative statement, just one to help guide thoughts and decisions as you prepare to reach people for Christ.

If we hold on to this phrase as we engage the Advent story and think honestly about God's method of saving and redeeming the world in Christ, maybe we can catch a vision of how we can participate in God's rescue plan and prepare for His return.

Jesus comes poor and powerless. He comes humbly; He comes as a minimalist. He comes needy and he comes crying. Not as a powerful king, flashy entertainer or crafty politician but as a baby. A BABY! In this form, He begins His redemptive mission to win the world to Himself and to make all things new.

In Christ's birth, we get a glimpse of God's means. If this is how God is choosing to win and redeem the world, maybe this is also how He wants to shape our lives. He helps us see that when we are poor, meek, powerless, persecuted, humble, merciful and pure in heart, we are actually blessed and participants in His means of redemption.

As we prepare for the coming of Christ in His birth and His return, are we trying to gain power, put on a flashy show or accumulate lots of stuff? Or are we giving away our stuff to those in need? Creating space for the poor and powerless in our lives? Are we trying to align our lives more with the humble and minimal path that God chose in the manger or are we do something very different?

How might we conform more to God's means of saving the world
and less to the means of our culture?

Meditation ::.

"The fruit will show that repentance has been genuine. The waring echoes down the years, and must be taken to heart by all the baptized today. We cannot presume that because we have shared in the great Christian mystery, the new Exodus coming through the water of baptism with all that it means, God will automatically be happy with us even if we show no signs of serious repentance. Of course, Christian living is far more than simply repentance but it is not less. All spiritual advance begins with turning away from what is hindering our obedience. If John were to come down your street with a megaphone, what would he be saying?"

Luke For Everyone, N.T. Wright

Theologian N.T. Wright translates the first part of Luke 3:8 like this: "You'd better prove your repentance by bearing the proper fruit!" As we prepare for Advent, I want to connect and even equate the fruit of repentance with the fruit of preparedness. John the Baptist seems to connect these two things as well. The fruit that grows from a repentant life that has turned body and mind toward God and His mission will be the same fruit growing from the life of a disciple who is truly preparing for Christ's return.

What will this fruit look like? As we talked about, you will seek justice, you will love mercy and you will walk humbly with the God of scripture as you await His return. This is preparedness for John. Remember that during Advent we are called to make straight the path of the Lord. We need to be prepared to remember His coming in birth and to live a life of preparedness for His second coming. In the ways you go about preparing your heart, mind and surroundings for the return of Christ, you will see the fruit of authentic repentance and preparation.

Do you see the fruit of preparation in your own life?
If not, how is God calling you to repentance?

HOPE

ADVENT :: SUNDAY #3

Isaiah 61:1-4, 8-11 | 1 Thessalonians 5:16-24
Psalm 126 | John 1:6-8, 19-28

HOPE // Day 16
READING :: Luke 1:39-56

When we encounter hope, we sense an excitement and energy in the air. This is why hope is so often connected to the birth of a child. Hope anticipates, waits, prepares and stirs with excitement. If you've ever had a baby born in your family, you probably understand this.

I love the picture that we get in Luke 1:39-56: Two pregnant women, literally filled with hope! They see each other for the first time and, if you read the story carefully and picture the scene in your mind, place yourself in the room; you can sense the excitement and energy. These two women who should not be able to have kids—one because she is too old and one because she is too young, a virgin even—greet each other with great affection. Though separated by many years of age, they're family, and now they are sharing a profound and God-filled experience. They're having babies! The Holy Spirit fills the place and the people as they see each other and embrace; even the babies in their bellies start jumping and dancing. Mary bursts into song, "My soul glorifies the Lord and my spirit rejoices in God my savior."

Hope has entered and filled the room.

During Advent, we retell and relive this story of hope coming on the scene, a story about the Word becoming flesh and moving into the neighborhood, as Eugene Peterson says in The Message (John 1:14). Hope is coming to your house, your street, to your neighborhood, in the form of a baby! Everything will be different! Tomorrow won't look the same as today! What's in Mary's belly will change the world and everybody in it. Even the unborn babies know it.

Advent is a time of this toe-curling, breath-catching hope. We are filled with hope knowing that Jesus is coming into the world and that He will come again to put the broken pieces back together and make all things new. So we wait, we prepare, we hope—we stay awake to all that God is doing and will do.

Can you think of a time when you felt the
energy and excitement connected to hope?

One book that helps me reflect on hope during Advent is N.T. Wright's masterpiece *Surprised By Hope*. In the introduction, he asks two questions: "What is the ultimate Christian hope?" and "What hope is there for change, rescue, transformation, new possibilities within the world in the present?" Here is how N.T. Wright responds.

"If Christian hope is for God's new creation, for 'new heavens and new earth,' and if that hope has already come to life in Jesus of Nazareth, then there is every reason to join the two questions together. And if that is so, we find that answering the one is also answering the other. I find that to many—not least, many Christians—all this comes as a surprise: both that the Christian hope is surprisingly different from what they had assumed and that this same hope offers a coherent and energizing basis for work in today's world."

This is obviously a deep and profound conversation. Essentially N.T. Wright is saying that we often think our hope is heaven—that someday we will leave this world and life will be what we had always "hoped" it would be. But during Advent and Christmastide, we remember that Jesus was born as a human. As Wright says, "Hope has already come to life in Jesus of Nazareth..." Jesus is our hope, helping us know that salvation came to this world, not some far-away place and not for some long-awaited day. Jesus is our hope for today, not just for someday.

Advent and Christmastide help us remember God wanted to save our world, and us, and that's why He came. This is Christian hope.

> Have you ever been tempted to think your hope was found
> in escaping this broken world by going to heaven someday?
> How might Jesus bring hope to your life today?

Paul proclaims that faith and love spring from hope. Somehow, when we have hope, we have the ability to see past this day's despair and disaster and, through Christ, see a tomorrow full of the potential of our faith and love come alive. Then we can begin to participate with the creative energy of resurrection and new life that only Christ, our hope, can give to our tomorrows.

I once heard that hope is a door opened to the future. The opposite of hope is despair, and despair is all about only being able to see today's negativity and unruly circumstances. Hope is someone, maybe even a baby in a manger, being able to open a door that enables you to see a better tomorrow.

We have all seen classic stories of hope in movies like *Lean on Me*, *Dangerous Minds, Coach Carter* and many others. In these films, a teacher goes into a school full of broken kids living in broken circumstances. Until now, the kids have seen violence, addiction and self-preservation as their only options. But the teacher steps in and helps them to see another, better way. Students realize that if they work hard, study and participate in the world of school and grades and tests, they can have a different future than everyone around them. In essence, the teachers open a door to the future for the troubled students. They give hope.

Philosopher Soren Kierkegaard says, "Hope becomes a passion for what is possible."

During Advent, we are the students living as if today is all we have and nothing is ever going to get better. But we are reminded that a child is on the way. Hope is about to fill the room and the world. Our tomorrows are full of possibilities because this baby who is hope is on his way, once in His birth and finally and definitely in His second coming.

Have you ever witnessed a story of hope like the one mentioned in the movies above?

Who do you know who might be caught in despair?
How can you help them see another, better way?

Much like the birth of Christ revealed a great light coming into the world, the Transfiguration of Jesus reveals for a second time that Christ is the light shining brightly into our world. The disciples needed to turn their faces away from the brightness as, for a moment, Jesus lifted the veil between this world and the world to come. It is this light, that is Christ that gives us hope and helps us navigate the difficult circumstances of our world.

Rowan Williams in his book, *The Dwelling of the Light: Praying with Icons of Christ*, meditates on an icon of the Transfiguration and says this:

"In the strength of that glimpse (seeing this light), things become possible. We can confront today's business with new thoughts and feelings, reflect on our sufferings and our failures with some degree of hope — not with a nice and easy message of consolation but with the knowledge that there is a depth to the world's reality and out of that comes the light which will somehow connect, around and in Jesus Christ, all the complex, painful, shapeless experience of human beings."

He continues, "Peter, James and John are allowed to see Christ's glory so that when they witness his anguish and death they may know that these terrible moments are freely embraced by the God-made-human who is Jesus, and held within the infinite depth of life."

In the same way we see in Jesus' birth, we also see in His mysterious transfiguration that He is the light of the world, the hope in our present darkness. He sheds light on our darkness and despair as well as the darkness and despair that he and his friends will go through when he is crucified.

We see this begin at His birth, we catch a bright reminder in the Transfiguration and we wait for the light's final work in Christ's return. Where there is light, there is hope. This is true in the most difficult and dark circumstance. Christ truly is the light of the world.

When have you seen a glimpse of Christ's light in your life?
How has it given you hope?

Meditation ::.

"Come, Lord Jesus" is a leap into the kind of freedom and surrender that is rightly called the virtue of hope. The theological virtue of hope is the patient and trustful willingness to live without closure, without resolution, and still be content and even happy because our satisfaction is now at another level, and our source is beyond ourselves. We are able to trust that he will come again, just as Jesus has come into our past, in our private dilemmas and into our suffering world. Our Christian past then becomes our Christian prologue, and "Come, Lord Jesus" is not a cry of desperation but an assured shout of cosmic hope."

Preparing For Christmas, Richard Rohr

Many of us only ask for Jesus to come when we're in trouble. Or, we call His name out of frustration, which doesn't really have much to do with Jesus anyway. Richard Rohr speaks of hope as a virtue. He encourages us that our Advent words "Come, Lord Jesus" can be more than frustration or a plea of desperation. They can cultivate a hope greater than anything our own efforts can accomplish and openness to a future we can't imagine.

For hope to become a virtue, it must be something we regularly embrace and lean into in our daily lives—not letting our circumstances stir despair but keeping our eyes fixed on Jesus, the author and perfecter of our faith. In our usage of the Advent mantra "Come, Lord Jesus," we invite Jesus, our hope, into every potential outcome and embrace whatever future God chooses to bring our way.

During Advent and Christmastide, we remember that God will often do things in ways we could never have guessed, and all we can do is say "Bring it on, Jesus"—or, more properly put, "Come, Lord Jesus."

Are you open and prayerful to anything and everything that Jesus might bring your way as you pray "Come, Lord Jesus"?

Meditation ::.

"This hope makes the Christian Church a constant disturbance in human society, seeking as the latter does to stabilize itself into a continuing city. It makes the Church the source of continual new impulses towards the realization of righteousness, freedom and humanity here in the light of the promised future that is to come. This church is committed to 'answer for the hope' that is in it (1 Peter 3:15). It is called in question 'on account of the hope and resurrection of the dead' (Acts 23.6). Wherever that happens, Christianity embraces its true nature and becomes a witness of the future of Christ."

Theology of Hope, Jurgen Moltman

In our passage for today, Peter reminds us that we are to have an answer for the hope that is in us. The preface to this idea is that you have hope in you! As we discussed earlier, this isn't something you are simply given, but instead this hope is Christ. He is our living, breathing hope!

1 Peter 3 indicates that this hope will be so visible in your life that people will ask questions. They will want to know why you see a future, a tomorrow, when there is so much poverty and despair in today. They will want to know why, when the crooked path so greatly traveled is available, you opt for the straight and honest path. They will question why you choose the road of love when most choose the winding road of self. 1 Peter guarantees you will be questioned and even slandered. But we have an answer for our hopeful behavior that this world finds so disturbing. We have an answer for the hope in us that enables us to be more authentically human and to care for our broken world.

Our hope is Jesus, the person who is coming as a baby to show the world the very heart and action of God. Our hope is also the promise of his return.

Do you live in such a radically hopeful and abundant way
that people call into question the hope that is in you?
What is your answer for the hope you have?

AWAKE

ADVENT :: SUNDAY #4

2 Samuel 7:1-11, 16 | Romans 16:25-27
Psalm 89:1-4, 19-26 | Luke 1:26-38

"But about that day or hour no one knows, neither the angels in heaven, nor the Son, but only the Father. Beware, keep alert; for you do not know when the time will come. It is like a man going on a journey, when he leaves home and puts his slaves in charge, each with his work, and commands the doorkeeper to be on the watch. Therefore, keep awake—for you do not know when the master of the house will come, in the evening, or at midnight, or at cockcrow, or at dawn, or else he may find you asleep when he comes suddenly. And what I say to you I say to all: Keep awake!" —Mark 13:32-37, NRSV

This last week of Advent is fascinating. It's a week pregnant with excitement. The journey is about to reach its peak and a party is in order! But it's also bit scary, as this baby who will change everything is on His way. Most of us have calendars, and if we pay close attention, we can know the exact day and time He will come—but beware! The special day falls on a different day of the week every year. If we're not careful and awake to what's going on, it sneaks up on us like many birthdays, anniversaries and holidays often do.

This week, I want to lean into the biblical images of the wise men, the shepherds and the disciples who are awake (but sometimes asleep) to all that God is doing in their world. I hope they can serve as our inspiration to be ready to receive the unexpected in the midst of ordinary life. Let's take a deep breath and really think about our awareness of God's coming in our lives and circumstances. Are we awake to what God is up to, or are we too distracted and busy to notice, missing the moments when God is breaking into our lives?

I love the passage that starts us off this week. Some versions of Mark 13:32-37 conclude with the words "Watch!²" or "Stay alert!³" or "Stay awake.⁴" I might even translate it "don't fall asleep." But I love how the NRSV ends emphatically with the words "Keep awake!" (I added the exclamation mark myself, but I think it fits.)

That's our challenge this week: *KEEP AWAKE!* The plane could land any minute now. You better be ready!

Are you awake and ready for the coming of Christ,
not just on Christmas Day but also in every moment of your life?

In Matthew 2, we meet the wise men. There may have been three wise men, as typically portrayed in the retelling of the story, but some people think there may have been 12 or even more. We also refer to these men as Magi, which many people think could mean magicians or astronomers. Whatever their occupation or number, they were going about their business, doing what wise men do when they see a star. They were awake! Awake to what was going on; awake to what God was doing. They saw the star and moved to participate in what God was up to in the world!

In spite of all the fascinating details surrounding the wise men, I want us to focus on the fact that they were awake to signs, awake to the movement of God and the circumstances He was putting into place to give hope and restoration to the world in the form of a baby—Jesus. I've missed enough signs in my life to know even if you're looking for them, you need to be awake, aware and alert. Even if you're driving on an open road, it can be easy to miss the signs. If you've ever been lost on a road trip and took a wrong turn, you know exactly what I'm talking about.

Are you awake to the small signs, the mysterious occurrences in your daily life? In many ways, as Christmas approaches, everything seems normal for the wise men. We do this every year. We go to church every week. But are we still searching the skies like the wise men must have been, and searching for the ways God is breaking into our lives, into our Christmas festivities and into our world? The wise men set an example for us to take action when we see God is up to something. This could be a normal week like any other. Or, it could be a week where God, in a fresh way, breaks into our world and reveals Himself to us!

How could you be more intentionally awake
to what God is doing in your life this last week of Advent?

The shepherds play a central role in the Christmas story. We've all seen the children parading around with their staffs and bathrobes in church Christmas pageants. But did you know that in biblical times, the job of a shepherd only sometimes went to young boys? Think of David shepherding in the fields. However, most of the time, this job went to sinister types running from the law, like Moses, who was a fugitive after murdering an Egyptian. Shepherds would try to hide out in the fields where no one could find them and they could live anonymously among the sheep. You can at least trust sheep, right? Shepherds were often the outcasts of society. They were ignored and marginalized. They probably even smelled bad. But guess what? "An angel of the Lord appeared to them, and the glory of the Lord shone around them, and they were terrified. But the angel said to them, 'Do not be afraid. I bring you good news...'"

No wonder they were freaked out! These shepherds weren't used to receiving attention, especially supernatural attention. But the angel told them, "Don't be afraid. I've got good news for you and for everybody!" That particular night, the shepherds probably weren't ready to be found. They probably weren't ready for the Lord to break into their under-the-radar lifestyle and shine a huge spotlight on them. They surely weren't expecting to be the messengers of God's great news to the world. But once again, God chose the least likely individuals to celebrate, participate and proclaim what He was doing in the world. He handpicked the shepherds to spread the good news of His coming, and they responded wholeheartedly.

Maybe, like the shepherds, you feel like you're the least qualified person for God to use to spread His news. You aren't even expecting Him to come into your life and reveal Himself to you at all. We all feel that way sometimes. But when God does come—and He will!—it's our responsibility to be awake and respond! It's not about you and your qualifications. It's about God and His grace, using anybody and everybody who is awake and willing. If that's you, be ready. Be awake!

Have you ever felt like you were unqualified to be used by God?
Are you open to God coming into your life
and using you to spread the good news of His coming?

41

AWAKE // DAY 26
READING :: Matthew 26:36-46

Have you ever fallen asleep while you were praying? Or, have you ever been distracted and so wrapped up in other thoughts, to-do lists and issues that you never finished your prayer—you just got up and went on with your day? We are constantly awake to all the pressing issues and problems that need solving, but asleep to the things God might have wanted to chat with us about. At least, that happens to me too often.

As I read today's scripture, I want to come down hard on the disciples for their lack of alertness to what is happening. How can they just fall asleep? But if I'm honest, I am one of those disciples. I fall asleep more often than I stay awake. I miss the signs more often than I follow His direction. I too often give in to my flesh rather than stand up for my faith.

Jesus even instructs the disciples in verse 41, "Stay awake and in prayer so that you don't fall into temptation. The spirit is willing, but the flesh is weak." A part of us desires to be awake and alert to everything God is doing. But the other part is weak, distracted and tired, and simply wants to go to sleep.

Christmas often lulls us into an exhausted stupor. There are presents to buy, decorations to hang, trees to cut down, parties to host, more parties to attend, food to cook, relatives to keep happy. I could go on, but you get the idea. In the midst of the hustle and bustle, it's pretty easy to fall asleep to what God is doing. A baby is quietly born. God is taking on skin and moving into the neighborhood, putting His plan into action. Yet we are asleep to it. We're awake to our lists and distracted desires—and asleep to the activity of God. We, like the disciples, are in danger of missing an opportunity to participate in what God is doing right here, in our homes and schools and communities. So I remind you of Jesus' words, "Stay awake and in prayer."

How can you stay awake to God and His activity this Christmas and shrug off the exhausting distractions of the holiday season?

Meditation ::.

"Come, Lord Jesus," the Advent mantra, means that all of Christian history has to live out of a kind of deliberate emptiness, a kind of chosen non-fulfillment. Perfect fullness is always to come, and we do not need to demand it now. This keeps the field of life wide open and especially open to grace and to a future created by God rather than ourselves. This is exactly what it means to be "awake" as the gospel urges us! We can also use other words for Advent: aware, alive, attentive, alert, awake are all appropriate! Advent is, above all else, a call to full consciousness."

Preparing For Christmas, Richard Rohr

This week, we've looked at characters in the Bible who have been aware, alive, alert, and awake to what God was doing in and around them. There is intentionality to this kind of alertness. It can be hard work. But, like so many things, if you practice and regularly incorporate disciplines like alertness into your life, they become second nature.

N.T. Wright talks about this idea in his book, *After You Believe*. He says that after you believe in Jesus, many things are foreign, odd, and even contrary to your natural tendencies. But after you begin to practice spiritual disciplines, they become incorporated into your life. They become things you wind up doing without even thinking about it. Waiting, hoping, and being fully awake to God's work are all virtues that we don't naturally practice in our lives. They are hidden by our busy schedules, social media, television, and the demands of our teachers, parents and friends. We must cultivate and incorporate alertness into our lives until it does become second nature, or we risk living our lives asleep and missing out on God's plan.

The work of Advent—being aware, alive, attentive, alert, and awake, the call to "full consciousness" as Rohr puts—is something we specially strive for during this season. But if we carry one thing with us beyond Advent into ordinary time, let it be this practice of living awake. With the help of the Spirit of God, we will remain awake as we continue to wait on the coming of Christ in all the days of our lives.

How can you help your Advent practice of alertness become second nature in your life?

Meditation ::.

"It is Advent again. In his sermon this morning, Oscar Uzin said: 'Be alert, be alert, so that you will be able to recognize your Lord in your husband, your wife, your parents, your children, your friends, your teachers, but also in all that you read in the daily papers. The Lord is coming, always coming. Be alert to his coming.' When you have ears to hear and eyes to see, you will recognize him at any moment of your life. Life is Advent; life is recognizing the coming of the Lord."

Prayer

"Lord Emmanuel, Prince of Peace, let us be especially alert to your coming during this Advent. As a parent listens for the cry of an infant, as a sailor watches for land, as an astronomer scans the skies, as a doctor watches for signs of returning health, let us be attentive to your arrival. Let not our pride and arrogance blind us and put us to sleep. Give us the endurance to be true watchers of the night as we journey through this Advent. Amen."

Advent and Christmas, Henri Nouwen

Can you imagine a sailor who hasn't seen land in weeks gazing off into the horizon, desperately hoping for a glimpse of land? Or a doctor examining a patient, searching for signs that his treatment is working so he can restore the sick person to health and vitality? These metaphors from Henri Nouwen are perfect for the end of our Advent journey. They capture the heart-pounding desire we feel as we wait, prepare and hope in the day of God's coming. Even if you can't muster the strength of that desire, let this prayer be your guide. Spend a few extra moments today reflecting on your wait, awakening to all God has done in your life this Advent.

How has God been born in new ways in your life this Advent?
Where have you seen him coming to life?

CHRISTMASTIDE

Christmastide :: SUNDAY #5

Isaiah 61:10-62:3 | John 1:1-18
Galatians 3:23-25;4:4-7 | Psalm 147 or 147:13-21

READING :: A Chronological Reading
of the Christmas Story
Matt 1:18a — Luke 1:26-40 — Luke 1:56 — Matt 1:18b —
Luke 2:1-38 — Matt 2:1-23 — Luke 2:39-40

Today, Christmas, is the culmination of our waiting, watching, preparing and planning. Our hope has come alive! Jesus is here. Take a deep breath and reflect on the supremely important work God has done.

Today is also a feast day. A festival is in order! It is good and right for God's people to celebrate His presence among us, as one of us.

Today's verses give a full and clear telling of the Christmas story. Sit down with your family, friends, neighbors or whomever you may be celebrating with, and ponder this story.

Head over to the Advent Web guide for a link to an audio dramatization of the Christmas story as well.

Christ has come, Alleluia!

Meditation ::.

"He looks like anything but a king. His face is prunish and red. His cry, though strong and healthy, is still the helpless and piercing cry of a baby. And he is absolutely dependent upon Mary for his wellbeing.

Majesty in the midst of the mundane. Holiness in the filth of sheep manure and sweat. Divinity entering the world on the floor of a stable, through the womb of a teenager and in the presence of a carpenter.

She touches the face of the infant—God. How long was your journey!

This baby had overlooked the universe. These rags keeping him warm were the robes of eternity. His golden throne room had been abandoned in favor of a dirty sheep pen. And worshiping angels had been replaced with kind but bewildered shepherds.

Meanwhile, the city hums. The merchants are unaware that God has visited their planet. The innkeeper would never believe that he had just sent God into the cold. And the people would scoff at anyone who told them the Messiah lay in the arms of the teenager on the outskirts of their village. They were all too busy to consider the possibility.

Those who missed His Majesty's arrival that night missed it not because of evil acts or malice; no, they missed it because they simply weren't looking.

Little has changed in the last two thousand years. Has it?"

God Came Near, Max Lucado

Spend 15 minutes today doing Lectio Divina, a sacred prayerful reading of the story. Let the words come alive in your imagination—the sights and sounds, the smells and the textures of Christ's birth. Place yourself in the story. What would you have experienced? Like Mary, ponder all these things in your heart (Luke 2:19).

Head over to the Advent Web Guide to find guidance on how to do Lectio Divina.

I didn't always see John 1 as a Christmas story. There's no baby, no manger, no wise men or shepherds. But it's a Christmas story nonetheless.
"The Word became flesh and made his dwelling among us. We have seen his glory, the glory of the one and only Son, who came from the Father, full of grace and truth." (John 1:14)

John 1 tells the Christmas story from an entirely new perspective. It's big; it's cosmic. It starts before the world is even formed with the Word. Then we see that the connection to Genesis, "in the very beginning," and it all peaks with the Word becoming flesh, which is the birth of Christ and then it continues on into eternity.

N.T. Wright says the following about John's version of the Christmas story: "John is saying two things simultaneously in his prologue (two hundred things, actually, but I'll concentrate on two): First, that the Incarnation of the eternal Word was the event for which the whole of creation had been waiting all along; second, that creation and even the people of God were quite unready for this event. Jew and Gentile alike, upon hearing of this strange Word, cast anxious glances at one another, like the celebrity and the headmaster hearing a little boy telling the truth in a language they didn't understand.

"That is the puzzle of Christmas. John's prologue is designed to stay in the mind and heart throughout the subsequent story. Never again in the Gospel of John is Jesus referred to as 'the Word,' but we are meant to look at each scene—the call of the first disciples, the changing of water into wine, the confrontation with Pilate, the Crucifixion, and the Resurrection—and think to ourselves: This is what it looks like when the Word becomes flesh. Or, if you like: Look at this man of flesh and learn to see the living God."[5]

Has your Advent journey prepared you to see this cosmic perspective of the Christmas story? To witness Jesus, full of grace and truth, being born into our world and growing up to show us how to see the living God making His home among us?

In Max Lucado's book, *Cosmic Christmas*, he writes from the perspective of the angels and what they would have witnessed and experienced as God took on flesh and made His dwelling among us. Let these words stir your imagination.

Meditation ::.

"We were a wreath of Light around the stable, a necklace of diamonds around the structure. Every angel had been called from his post for the coming, even Michael. None doubted God would, but none knew how He could, fulfill His promise.

'I've heated the water!'

'No need to yell, Joseph, I hear you fine.'

Mary would have heard had Joseph whispered. The stable was even smaller than Joseph had imagined, but the innkeeper was right—it was clean. I started to clear out the sheep and cow, but Michael stopped me. "The Father wants all of creation to witness the moment."

'Aaaiieee!'

Mary gripped Joseph's arm with one hand and a feed trough with the other. The thrust in her abdomen listed her back, and she leaned forward.

'Is it time?' Joseph panted.

She shot back a glance, and he had his answer.

Within moments the Awaited One was born. I was privileged to have a position close to the couple, only a step behind Michael. We both gazed into the wrinkled face of the infant. Joseph had placed hay in a feed trough, giving Jesus His first bed.

All of God was in the infant. Light encircled His face and radiated from His tiny hands. The very glory I had witnessed in His throne room now burst through His skin.

I felt we should sing but did not know what. We had no song. We had no verse. We had never seen the sight of God in a baby. When God had made a star, our words had roared. When He had delivered His servants, our tongues had flown with praise. Before His throne, our songs never ended.

But what do you sing to God in a feed trough?"

It's the fifth day of Christmas—has anybody given you five golden rings? I confess I never knew there was any merit to the silly song "The Twelve Days of Christmas." It wasn't until just a few years ago that I realized there were actually 12 days Christmas on the liturgical calendar. It's not just the lyrics to a kids' song. Advent always precedes the 12 days of Christmas.

Some people try to give special significance to each day, even connecting each line of the song to a hidden message, like three hens standing for the three members of the Trinity. They argue that the song was used to subversively teach Christian doctrine when the Church was being persecuted. I like that idea, but there isn't much to back it up. In addition to the several feast days during the 12 days of Christmas, these 12 days are generally about celebrating what God has done. They allow us to embrace the story, as we've done in the first four readings this week, and to give thanks for the work of God in our world through His son, our savior Jesus Christ.

Joan Chittister, in her book *The Liturgical Year*, enhances our perspective as we journey through these 12 days:

"The Christmas season, if we see it as a whole rather than as an isolated event (and, in our age, a totally distorted and even misleading conception of the feast), it can ignite the spark that will lead through the darkness of our own lives every day of the year. It is the light of Christmas within us that will take us, if we have the insight to cling to it, beyond a fairytale rendering of the great truths of the faith to an understanding of what all the dark days of life are about."

She continues,

"Christmas is larger than a baby in a manger. Christmas is the coming of a whole new world. More than that, it is what makes that world possible."

How are you choosing to celebrate Jesus, not just on Christmas Day but also during the 12 Days of Christmas? And beyond?

Meditation ::.

"O Son of God and Son of Man,
Thou wast incarnate, didst suffer, rise, ascend for my sake;
Thy departure was not a taken of separation but a pledge to return;
Thy Word, promises, sacraments, show thy death until thou come again.
That day is no horror to me, for thy death has redeemed me,
thy Spirit fills me, thy love animates me, thy Word governs me.
I have trusted thee and thou hast not betrayed my trust;
waited for thee, and not waited in vain."

A meditation from the book, *Valley of Vision*

Advent has come to an end, and we are no longer focusing on waiting and hoping in the same way we did during previous weeks. As we celebrate the fact that Jesus was born and that He came to us, we don't lose sight of the fact that He will also come again. What we have experienced during Christmas, the celebration it stirred, and the hope it brought to fullness, we will experience again with even more jubilation when Christ returns.

We talk about the Second Coming much like how we have talked about His first coming, how the light has come and will come into the world. If we look around, we can see the light has a lot of shining left to do. So we participate and celebrate in the light that is Jesus, but we also wait for His return. On that day, Jesus will shine His light brightly into all the corners and crevices of our dark world. And this light will make all things new. We both celebrate the light that has come and continue to wait for the light that will come.

As you celebrate Christ's coming during Christmastide, how are you keeping in mind that He will come again?

Meditation ::.

"In other words, if he (Jesus) were to come today, he could very well do what you do. He could very well live in your apartment or house, hold down your job, have your education and life prospects, and live within your family, surroundings, and time. None of this would be the least hindrance to the eternal kind of life that was his by nature and becomes available to us through him. Our human life, it turns out, is not destroyed by God's life but is fulfilled in it and in it alone.

The obviously well-kept secret of the 'ordinary' is that it is made to be a receptacle of the divine, a place where the life of God flows."

The Divine Conspiracy, Dallas Willard

By now, the truth should be sinking into your mind and heart: God has come in flesh and blood and made His dwelling among us. As Dallas Willard says, the ordinary has become the receptacle of the divine. I love that. The Christmas story truly is a divine conspiracy.

So this Christmastide, are we letting the life of God flow through our ordinary lives and activities, or are we, as we too often do, relegating God to church and our Christian activities? Are we active participants in the divine conspiracy no matter where we find ourselves?

How can you be an ordinary receptacle for the divine?
Think of three ordinary things you do
that you could turn into divine outlets.

Meditation ::.

"Whatever it is that God is about to do, it will be good news for the poor, bad news for the proud and the rich; it will be change, including changed economic and social relations. This was the expectation that Jesus himself picked up, when in terms almost identical to John's, he announced that 'the kingdom of heaven is near' and then more precisely:

"'The Spirit of the Lord is upon me, because he has anointed me to proclaim good news to the poor. He has sent me to proclaim liberty to the captives and recovering of sight to the blind, to set at liberty those who are oppressed, to proclaim the year of the Lord's favor' (Luke 4:18, 19)."

The Original Revolution, John Howard Yoder

I've always been a big fan of the idea of revolution—this idea that God's people are called to stand up in the middle of our culture and context and go a different way. I believe God leads us in this different way. Hopefully, as you have journeyed through this book, you've picked up on some of the revolutionary postures we are called to live. Postures like waiting, hoping, giving, caring for the poor and being open to the divine. These are just some of the postures we are called live into and that we learn about as Christ followers during Advent and Christmastide.

I once heard Rob Bell say, "At the heart of the Christian faith is a disruption." You see, God breaks in and disrupts our me-focused life time and time again. He breaks in and disrupts our selfish, off-centered lives as well. As we learned yesterday, He takes the ordinary and fills it with the divine. God in Christ invites us into this disruptive activity, to participate in His revolution. This revolution is clearly displayed during Advent and Christmastide.

There are many ways for us to participate in God's disruptive revolution, but I want to give you a challenge:

As a family or church community, take inventory of what you received this Christmas. Then, for every item you received, give away one item to the poor, to the marginalized, to anybody with less. Be fair. Take into account not only the quantity but also the value. Give as much as you received as a way to participate in God's revolution.

Love came down on Christmas Day. You've probably heard this idea generalized in songs about having a happy Christmas and illustrated with hot chocolate, toasty fires and snowmen.

Don't get me wrong—I like all those things! The first Christmas I lived in Texas, I was absolutely terrified that I wouldn't get a white Christmas as I always had, growing up in the Chicago area. But it snowed: a Christmas Day miracle! My two-year-old son and I ran outside and made snow angels, and when we came inside, cold and dripping, my wife had mugs of steaming hot chocolate ready and waiting! It was awesome!

As great as they might be, though, our romanticized white Christmas notions aren't the real essence of love coming down on Christmas. Instead, the love that came down on Christmas was Jesus Himself, God wanting to show in the flesh what it looks like to be a God with a real heartbeat, who moves into the neighborhood, who loves on the ground. Christmas love is about embracing real people, not just lofty ideas or great theories.

We see God's love in a unique, human way on Christmas Day. We know God is love, but this truth moves from being an idea, a kind of theology that we can study about in class, to an image we can see and an example we can follow. Love comes down on Christmas Day so that we might see it, experience it and ultimately live it.

Because we have this example to follow, love starts to make sense. When we embrace the birth of Christ—the incarnation of God—patience and kindness begin to come alive in our hearts. Characteristics like humility and honoring our neighbor, serving and forgiving our friends and enemies, they all start to stick. Christmas is the perfect time to begin to live out our beliefs with our lives.

How has your journey through Advent and into Christmas begun to produce in you the love of God for the world?

Meditation ::.

"I wonder, if we were to stop people at random on the street on December 24th and ask them what they want most of Christmas, how many would say, 'I want to see Jesus'?

I believe that the single most important consideration during the sacred season of Advent is intensity of desire. Paraphrasing the late Rabbi Abraham Heschel, 'Jesus Christ is of no importance unless he is of supreme importance." An intense inner desire is already the sign of his presence in our hearts. The rest is the work of the Holy Spirit."

Reflections for Ragamuffins, Brennan Manning

I love that the meditation above lets us hear from two great voices of the Christian faith. But even more than that, it begs us to reflect on our state of desire in an honest and open way.

I've heard Brennan Manning speak on a few different occasions. What struck me was that this humble man, full of faults and failures, wanted to want Jesus more and more.

During Christmastide, as we celebrate what we have been given may we not become satisfied. Instead, may this taste of the in-breaking of God into our lives and our world stir us to desire all the more that Christ would break into all our moments and into all our days.

It's like the end of a great festival, party or even church camp or conference. When the end draws near, we begin to long for it to come around again. The experience cultivates a desire for more. You don't get satisfied. Instead, the bit you've tasted makes you want it all the more. It cultivates a greater desire more than it satisfies that desire.

> Is your Christmastide celebration stirring greater desire
> for the presence of Jesus in your life?

Our passage for today contrasts sharply with Isaiah 8, in which the Israelites have turned from God to mediums, spirits and fortunetellers. They have turned to the culture and to false Gods for answers to their darkness. They are walking in darkness ,but there is hope! A child is to be born.

As I reflect on Christmas and what it has become in our culture, I still see a glimmer of hope. I see this glimmer in the full churches and houses of worship on Christmas Day. Many see this as the problem, and I understand that. For these people wandering in the dark, looking for answers in anything and everything, church is just another place they stop once or twice a year for a quick answer or least some entertainment to temporarily brighten up their darkness.

But what if we, those who have been waiting and praying, preparing for this light to come into the world in the person of Jesus, were able to leverage this day to show wanderers the truth and beauty of Jesus, the light of the world? To proclaim that in Christ, the light has taken shape and can be embraced as Lord and friend, a constant light to our dark paths?

We need to show a searching world that in all the conflict, depression and darkness of life, Jesus is the light. This is not to dismiss or diminish the difficulty of life or to indicate that it will go away with the birth of Jesus in our lives. Rather, Jesus becomes light and hope in the middle of our darkness. He disarms the fear and oppression of darkness now until the day when His glorious light will come again to dispel it completely. Until then, He journeys with us, as a light to our rocky and dark paths.

Who do you need to share the love and light of Jesus with as you wrap up your Advent and Christmastide journey?

CHRISTMASTIDE // DAY 12
READING :: John 14:1-21

Meditation ::.

"JESUS IS THE WAY, the truth, and the life. In order for us to truly understand what it means to believe that Jesus is the truth, we have to know the beginning, the middle and the end of Jesus' life. By the way, the end in Jesus' story is also the beginning of his resurrection.

In order for us to know the truth, we have to follow Jesus' way – his action, his pattern of behavior in connecting with the power and powerless of his time, his challenges to the powerful and rich, his way of laying his life down for others, his way of entering into the destruction of human fear and emerging triumphantly with love and grace.

In order to discern the truth, we need to live a life patterned after Jesus' – his relationships with his humble and courageous earthly parents, his acceptance of his calling, his recognition of his divinity, his compassion for the powerless and poor, his sharing of his power and authority with his friends, his boldness to challenge the system with love, his sharing of God's abundance, his courage to face suffering and death, and his unshakable belief in the resurrection."

Discerning the Truth in a Diverse and Changing World, Erik H.F. Law[6]

Our Advent and Christmastide journey has officially drawn to a close. As with all the seasons of the church, this journey is intended to stir in us a love for God and virtues of the Christian, Jesus-following life.

During Advent, we have learned to wait, hope and prepare for the in-breaking of God in our world and lives. These virtues don't come naturally; they must be cultivated as we practice living lives shaped by the scripture— and most importantly the example of Jesus.

Jesus' example of choosing the most humble way took center stage during our journey. In His adult life we see His example of love, healing and compassion, but in His birth, the way he chose to enter the world, we see a quieter illustration of the character of Jesus.

We have seen the truth in a helpless baby, who, from the first breath of his incarnate life, began to set a model for us of the way things work in the Kingdom of God.

What examples has God showed you during this journey
and how can you live them out?

EPIPHANY

EPIPHANY

The Season of Epiphany begins after the Twelve Days of Christmas and continues until Lent, 40 days before Easter. What exactly is it, and how do we observe it? Well, we've all had an "aha" moment when the lights go on and everything makes sense. That's an epiphany. It can happen slowly, like when the lights are gradually turned up in a room, or suddenly, when everything goes from black to full color and light in a moment.

I've had epiphanies take place both ways but it's always God who turns on the light! He reveals Himself and makes it clear that life will never be the same. This experience is different for every individual, but it's all a revelation of God's self.

Thus, Epiphany is the season in the church calendar when we watch and listen as God is quietly—or sometimes not so quietly—revealed before us once again. Sometimes, even when we try hard to do so, we just don't see God in our everyday lives or in the events of our world. Epiphany gives us the time and resources to watch, wait, listen, look and be open to the revelation of God. Watching and waiting are practices we can intentionally carry over from our Advent journey because Epiphany is a season that reminds us God constantly wants to reveal Himself to us. He longs to turn on the lights, connect the dots and show us the way!

The Lectionary will guide us through three key Scriptures readings during Epiphany. We traditionally focus on the Magi, who literally had the bright light of a star turned on above them to reveal what God was doing in the world. We also consider the baptism of Jesus, which more fully reveals who Jesus is, the Son of God. The season concludes with pondering the story of the Transfiguration, the scene that gives us a glimpse at the pure radiance of Jesus, the light of the world, as He reveals Himself to some of the disciples. We looked at the Magi on page 40 and the Transfiguration on page 33, but Epiphany is a season to really explore these aspects of Jesus' story that reveal Him in new ways.

My hope is that this page is a send off and spring board into the season of Epiphany. Continue to focus on God being revealed in your life this season. Let that be your focus and prayer until Lent begins in just a few short months. Head on over to the Advent Web Guide to check out some verses and recommended reading for the Epiphany season. You'll even find a few video links.

May the Lord continue to reveal Himself to you as your journey of watching, waiting and preparing for the light becomes a season of revelation.

Notes:

1. www.youtube.com/watch?v=PzTYPeiiSpU
2. New International Version
3. Common English Bible
4. English Standard Version
5. N.T. Wright, What Is This Word? Web article, ChristianityToday. com, 12/21/2006. Head over to the Advent Web Guide for a link to the full article.
6. Weavings: A Journal of the Christian Spiritual Life, May/June/July 2013

web : www.erikwillits.com
blog : www.erikwillitsblog.com
email : erik@erikwillits.com
twitter : twitter.com/erikwillits
facebook : facebook.com/erikwillits
instagram : erikwillits